Cooking Through Colors

coloring book

Dr. Angela Banner Joseph

ISBN-13: 978-1943945108

ISBN-10: 1943945101

Publisher: Dr. Angela Marie Joseph, New York City, NY

Printed in the United States of America

Cover Design: Stanley Joseph Leslie

Illustration: Rituparna Chatterjee

This Book Belongs To

_____

Also by Dr. Angela Banner Joseph

Two Nickels Holding Up a Dollar

I AM

Yo Soy

Teaching Charlie the Value of a Dollar

Girls Breaking the Mold

Black Men in Their Words About America

For my mother Geraldine C. Banner in heaven, and nieces Samiya, Summer, Maleeya, Tifanny, and nephew Edwin Jr.